Contents

1

A VISION IN BLUE

Storm kelpies, sea kelpies, sea creatures.
The blue men of Minch
personify the sea,
Vikings and Picts
with Norwegian forest cats.
Shantel isles, Outer Hebrides,
Ireland, Scotland, ancestral waters.

The great whales and leviathans
call out in sonar speaking
the ancient wisdom
from the ocean depths.
Transformed into elements
Air, Water, Aquarius, and Pisces
we unite.

A vision to see the future
now manifested as destiny.
Summoned by a force
greater than ourselves,
the Creator,
for a universal purpose
to be fulfilled.
We united for a reason.

You are the air above the sea,
the dragonfly that knows
both air and water,
you lead.

I am the water,
deep blue sea,
that hears the whales and leviathan
songs of sonar, directional tides
with the moon and intuition
as my guide.

No need to fear.
We are here, united,
for a purpose greater than ourselves
for the people.

Listening to the heart,
Joy, Happiness, Peace, Love
I am here to help you for a reason,
and so are you.
See ya in the winners' circle!

2

FEELINGS . . . 49 RAINBOW LIGHTS

Dressed in your finest
from head to toe,
you went out that night
to laugh, love,
and dance the night away.
How dare you!

You're supposed to hide
behind closed doors
in fear and shame.
Never to go out in public,
live in secret.
Never to show
your true self
or be proud of who you are.
Never to laugh,
especially not out and loud.
Never to love,
to show that part of us
to the world

That's right.
We love, just like you,
we are Americans too!
Tonight, we bled
a river of tears and blood
to your door
and the world's.
We are 49 rainbow lights
shining bright in
all directions across this land.
Our mighty nation blinded
by this senseless act
of hate and violence.

That's right.

Tonight you finally saw
we are Americans
just like you.

<u>3</u>

LIKE A BLUE TRAIN: THE TIGER EXPRESS

She is a steam engine blue train.
The Tiger Express!
Full of steam and locomotion.
Hissing and jostling down the track.
Zipping along those rails,
clickety, clack!

Pounding miles and tracks
across the great state of Wisconsin,
Selfless in all that's required.
Pushing against the headwinds of time,
as steam rolls off her back.
Head down, on mission,
nothing can stop the Blue Train,
clickety, clack!

Down those blue line tracks,
The Tiger Express is
A fierce competitor,
full of strength and beauty.
Don't mistakenly underestimate
her stealth, power, and grace!

The Tiger Express
Zephyr of our time.
A cool blue ocean wave
on hardened waves of steel.
Rocking, rolling, rumbling
down the tracks. Oh, so fast,
clickety, clack!

What a sight to see,
the Tiger Express
blurring those blue lines.
Crisscrossing, zig zagging
those gerrymandered lines.

The greatest conductor of our time!

And when she pulls into the station
on the last lap at warp speed,
There's only the sound of applause,
No more steam on rails that
clickety, clack.

Victory has arrived!
All that hard work and
effort so that the people
can survive and thrive.

Riding the Blue train
on the Blue waves of steel.
She's the Tiger Express.

See ya at the depot, Tiger!

4

ROY G. BIV

Red is the color of blood shed
in Orlando tonight.
One man's hate and gun violence
silenced the world.

Orange is the color of the belly chakra.
We are sickened
to the pit of our stomachs.
We feel the pain
from this tragedy like no other,
and yet, all others before it too.

Yellow is the color of the sunrise,
as morning news cameras
splashed the horror
to the world before us,
never to be the same again.

Green is the color of the grass
where many laid in pain and fear.
Waiting to be rescued
from that place.

Blue is the sky,
we all looked up to that day,
asking our Creator, why???
How could this happen
to 49 people?

Indigo, the color of squad cars
ambulance flashing lights.
Frozen in our memories.
Lights without sirens.
No noise. Just silence.
Disbelief left in memory,
a wake.

Violet is the color purple.
A reminder of our past;
lavender lesbians
and pink triangles.
It's the color of our faith,
how we cloak
our religious leaders.
The name of a book, *The Color Purple*,
that taught America about hate.

ROY G BIV is our rainbow pride,
our people, our lives,
our community,
our American dream.
Life, liberty the
pursuit of happiness.
We all know what it stands for.
Where do you stand today?

5

TEAM BLUE'S RACEHORSE - DREAM ALLIANCE KNOWN AS TAMMY S. BALDWIN

She's Team Blue's racehorse,
dream alliance, of our times.
Born of humble bloodlines
and beginnings,
USA, Wisconsin,
Madison, Dane County,
and the green, green grass
of home.

She was the people's choice,
their chosen racehorse
for Team Blue,
like Dream Alliance
of Irish and Welsh descent too.

Innocent, full of life,
always giving, never asking
anything in return,
driven by a vision for her people.
the workers' chosen racehorse,
giving them a sense of pride!
Ownership and hope
for a better life!

The Team Blue racehorse
(aka dream alliance),
was born Tammy S. Baldwin.
She stood tall, lithe, strong
like a tiger ready to run!

She wasn't afraid
to look her people in the eyes
to see their thoughts,
hopes, dreams and fears.
So she ran the races

and won all the more!

At nine years old a setback,
she pulled up lame...
put out of the race.
They said it was touch n go,
she may never race again.
Hopes and dreams dashed,
or were they?

No one knew the tiger with
her fight and courage within.
This magnificent creature,
otherworldly, strange,
quirky, not like the rest!
Hope combined with science
and stem cell like rehab
brought her back to race
for all of our hopes and
dreams again.

Her dreams and her peoples'
dreams, allied, reborn,
with a vision connecting us all!
Thy will be done, not mine!

Her work began in earnest,
the comeback slow and steady.
She understood everything
that was said to her
in heaven and on earth.

The people's hopes and dreams
alive within her,
the racehorse from humble bloodlines
and beginnings
is a part of the family
she belongs to Wisconsin now.
To race for the dream alliance
and team blue.

Hooves pounding, dust
and dirt flying off the track,
heavy breathing, chuffs of air
challengers competing alongside her.
She's pulling ahead and
away from the pack.
She's looked straight into our eyes

as she speeds round the track,
saying, "I'm back and I'll see all
of you in the winner's circle!"

And, then, That's when we all
began to think
that our humble hopes and dreams,
pinned to her back,
could truly come true for team blue!

We would all ask our ancestors
and God for a miracle that day
40: 1 odds with some saying
it couldn't be done.
Yet it would be Fate
and Destiny come true!

She's paid her people back
many times and many a race,
but this one goal
is a fairytale come true.
It would be a woman
who raced for team blue!

I can see her now
coming off the track
with heat and steam
hissing off her back.
Strong, lithe, like a tiger.
Magnificent!
Heavy breathing, nostrils flared,
giving a sweet, throaty
chuff of air to all of us
standing in her glare,

"What's all the fuss about?"
She's made them proud
and recognized at last,
elation follows when
no one ever gave you a chance.
Her people celebrate,
an absolutely breathtaking victory!
A dream come true for Team Blue.
Everybody will know the story
of our Dream Alliance, Racehorse;
Tammy S.Baldwin, come true!

6

YOU ARE A BLUE STAR-SPANGLED DRAGONFLY

Little did I know, as I watched the waves
at the blue ocean
That the dolphin would rise up
and out of the deep blue sea
in a spiral dance to catch a glimpse of thee.
The beautiful blue star-spangled dragonfly
zipping across the blue sky.
A manifestation and dream come true
for Team Blue!

Like the waters
Reflecting and mirroring dreams unleashed
in the tides of blue.
Your metamorphosis into reality
for Team Blue comes true.
Glimmering, shimmering, iridescent blue.
That's you overhead,
Performing amazing feats
as a skilled aerialist acrobat in flight.

You've rallied a squadron
of blue star-spangled dragonflies,
known as Team Blue.
All in flight to help and support you.
With stealth and speed,
they are all aerial acrobats too.
On a mission in flight for you and Team Blue.
The blue squadron in the air is a call to action
With a goal of greater good for all,

Freedom!
Your blue eyes sparkle as you fly overhead,
the dolphin rises in a spiral dance
to catch a glimpse of thee!
Magnificent!

7

BUTTERFLY

Roses are red,
Violets are blue,
What would it be like
to go out on a date with you?

Roses are red,
Violets are blue,
Seems I can't send real flowers
to a PO box for you?
So, I hope the paper type
with butterflies will do?

Roses are red,
Violets are blue,
Lupines are like me and
the Karner blue,
while Tiger Lilly and Swallowtail
remind me of you.

Roses are red,
Violets are blue,
Heart sings a song
about the dog and butterfly.
Guess I'm not alone
seeing things in the sky.

The Tiger swallowtail and
Karner blue butterfly
up in the air.
They like to fly.
We're getting older
I don't know why.

Oceans upon the sky.
Air + Water
The old man,
God, knows why.

8

DRAGONFLY SO FULL OF DESIRE

Dragonfly so full of desire.
Iridescent grace and beauty in flight.
Adept at great speeds,
an aerial acrobat in motion.
The deep, blue ocean ruled by the moon
and tides of emotions.

All that is feminine with compassion,
gently washing in and out to sea.
Mysterious blue water.

Fluid in form.
Ever adapting to obstacles in its path
with great powerful forces,
not to be contained.
To be observed, accepted, and adored
for its rhythmic, unconditional love.

Dragonfly's desire meets the waters
knowing the alchemy of air + water.
Ethereal, enchanting, passionate mist.
Tides and waves
gently rocking and pounding
obstacles and forces in the way.
Her depth mysterious and unknown.
Her intuition, a knowing leviathan sonar
in the depths of the blue sea.

Warm and swirling like a great bath,
drawn to soak luxuriously.
Sensuous and free floating,
surrounding and supporting
the one in need.
Water manifests the vision to be.
Calling out to the dragonfly
on the winds in prayer.

Gratitude.

9

HUMMINGBIRDS EVERYWHERE!

I see hummingbirds everyday.
I light your candle in the morning
and think of you listening
to my music with an open heart.

They are a paroxysm of joy
and bring magic on their
super beating wings.

To bring joy to others is a gift.
As it brings people together
and brings out the best in them.
Like the hummingbirds here,
I am surrounded by the beauty
of the driftless area and prairies.

I happily move about tasting
the nectar of this succulent life.
If the hummingbird holds
the bow of beauty,
inlaid with gold, silver, flowers,
peridots and pearls,
Surely, you hold the arrow
that has captured my heart.

With laughter, music, and
the Creator's gifts
laid open before me to see.
You energetically embrace
your gifts and
the highest aesthetics,

you move so swiftly about your days,
it sends my senses reeling.
The target is beauty,
so the hummingbird charts its course

to the tune of celestial music,
on a mission to spread joy.

I let my intuition be my guide
when I think of you
or I'm by your side,
it cannot be destroyed.
Joy, happiness, peace and love.

10

HUNTER'S MOON

Jupiter, Venus, Hunter's Moon
A trifecta is happening for all tonight.
Do you feel it?

It is said:
What you think you become.
What you feel you attract.
What you imagine, you create.

I am the dolphin,
circling fast beneath
the moonlit turquoise blue,
radiant water's surface.
Faster and faster,
I swim in a labyrinth pattern.
Counterclockwise then clockwise,
because I can.

Swiftly in pursuit.
I follow a sonar
intuitive drive.
Fast forward,
fast reverse,
full rudder stop.

Gazing above through
the iridescent glare,
searching all the while
to see if my
blue star-spangled dragonfly
is there.

I propel myself upwards,
as I sense a vision in blue
from the spiritual depths.
I've come to know

and rely upon as true blue.

I break free from the
water's surface at last.
Weaving and leaving
a blue wave in my path.
Vibrational energy
creating a ripple effect of
joy, happiness, peace and love.

It is then in the glint
I see my blue star-spangled dragonfly
high above.
An angel of joy with wings
lit like solar panels in
the hunter's moonlight,
she's a radiant beacon of love.

The connection is
clear and bright.
It's felt and understood
in the hunter's moonlight.
Gratitude for a gift of love
from the shining moon above.

11

IT'S OK LET YOUR FREAK FLAG FLY

Wishing you the wings to fly
my blue star-spangled dragonfly.
The vision to dream wildly
and boldly like a tiger's eye.

The heart to love deeply
as the ocean blue.
The spirit to embrace all beauty.

In life, we are all connected too.
High above in the ocean blue sky,
the blue star-spangled dragonfly
rides her precious steed,
the Pegasus unicorn.

Surrounded by her entourage
of little blue dragonflies.
She rides within the wings
of her Pegasus unicorn, safely.

Inside the Pegasus wings
there lies a heavenly kingdom
where angels serenade her
on morning glory harps.

She holds lightly onto the creature's
flowing mane, and rides safely
within her Pegasus wings.
Allowing her imagination to soar
freely through the sky.

Creating new galaxies
from her ocean blue sky vision.

12

RAINBOW TROUT

I'm a lil' fish rainbow trout,
swimming in the cool clear waters
of the black earth creek.

I've lived my years fully
swimming in the currents.
Even going upstream a few times.
I'm a lil' fish, Pisces, rainbow trout, Born
that way. Gay, as I like to say.

And, I've jumped for joy many a time
in the 61 years I've swam about.
But, never have I ever felt this
eternal connection with the AIR!

So, surely in my fishy being,
as I rose out of that cool, spring-fed,
water to feel you there,
as I jumped with joy, you were there.

As I leapt out of the safe,
familiar pool of water, you were there!
It was bright, surreal, refreshing, happy,
freeing and knowing all at once.

I met you Aquarius in the air
and it has forever changed me.
Swiftly, like the cool water flowing
downstream taking me in a new direction.
I welcome it and you!

Gratitude.

13

SIFTING & WINNOWING

Like grains of sand
we are all put through
the sifting and winnowing
process called life.
We are all put through
trials and tribulations.
No one escapes
the process.

Men and women.
All ages, colors and creed.
All abilities.
We are tested
to see if we can stand
the tests of time.
With faith to walk
the path alone.

It's true,
many will slip through
the cracks and holes
 as they are shaken
and sifted to their core.

They give into temptations
and quick fixes
for pain relief;
alcohol, drugs,
 sex, money, power.
Choosing to stay busy
 in the chaos,
drama and noise
versus silence.

It is in the letting go
and going with the flow

that we see the truth.

Those sifted that remain
have no fears.
For they know
they'll be
sifted and winnowed
again and again
by thy will.
To forever remain
in the basket
of eternal life.

14

STURGEON MOON

Tonight is the Sturgeon Moon.
Age of Aquarius.
The air and wind beneath my wings.

Tonight, you swim in the air,
a Sturgeon Moon.
Your prehistoric ancient wisdom
unfurls in the tidal wave of light,
surrounded by dark blue sea and sky.
Your playful adventurous side
on full display reflects your
beautiful luster, for all to see.
Orange, peach, then whiteness.
Your aura is clear from the heart
it's bright and light.

You swim in the air as I drum
from the depths of my ocean blue.
You radiate joy, happiness, peace and love.
Gently bathing all of thee, from far above.
A Sturgeon in the air, not in the sea?
How can it be?
Don't know, yet it seems to work
for you and me.
Totally grateful,
so let's just be, the air and the sea.

15

THE LONELY OAK

The lonely grown oak
with its ancient roots
spreading far and wide.
Its ancient DNA
anchoring this beauty
in the sunshine.
She's stood the test of time.
Only god knows why?

She's been through
many storms with
torrential rains,
even a 1000 year flood!
She's learned to be supple,
to be flexible and to adapt

from forceful winds
with trunk twisting blows.
To grow slowly
life and living is not a race.

She's survived
jolts of electricity
and lightning strikes
that shocked her
to the core.

A limb ravaged
in an instant
that forever altered
her silhouette
but not her
tenacious growth.

It's true
the deep wounds

are recorded
inside her body
so she will remember
the way to grow
beyond another day.

The aged open grown oak
with young leaves
flourishing.
All carefully nurtured
with the flow of
her water and zest for life.

The leaves tenderly open
spreading far and wide
giving all precious air
for life.
She's mastered the art
of life alone
and enjoys
the sunshine filled days
on the little hill
she calls home.

But she truly becomes
radiant and bright
when the winds kick up
tickling her with delight.
The gentle breeze
shakes her balance
and tussles her leaves.
She knows wind well,
like a good friend
and it knows
how to treat her
just right.

Together they sing
a song so pure
only the two can hear.
The song of water + air.
So the oak stands firmly
where she was rooted.

Growing more beautiful
with every sunlit day.
She now knows
water is life

so she gently gives
it to the air.

Together they create
a symphony for you
and me to just be.

16

THE WILD ONE; UN SAUVAGE

Born without a compass.
Full of curiosity.
Prone to adventures.
Independent to a fault.

Always searching,
scanning, reading signs
for something inside and out.

Led by songs heard in the deep
depths of her watery soul.
Or looking up to
the birds in the sky
that just so happen to fly on by.

Wandering and wondering
would she ever find her way home?
She often thought of her horse
leaving and telling him softly,
remember the way.
Then it just happened one day,
She found him and she was home.

17

WI BLUE SNOWFALL

I woke up slow today
to a new morning snow.
So grateful to see another day,
thanks to God for doing it his way.
Wondering how to start my day
after my coffee, and I pray.

Thinking about the ones
I love and hold so deep.
I hope and pray God will
gently blanket them with
his love as they start their day.

Checking the news feed
of my favorite Senator, Tammy B.
The fearless leader for Team Blue
giving her heart, sacrificing every day.
There's a reason you know,
It's bigger than me and you.

God made us like snowflakes
all unique in our own way
as he drops us to the ground.
Grateful I can see the beauty
in the blue snowfall
for that is where he places us,
for a reason greater than ourselves.

18

YOU ARE THE DRAGONFLY. I AM THE WATER.

The dragonfly hovered in the air,
above the ocean blue.
Attracted to the emerald, azure,
blue color of the water.
Desire and knowing exposed,

The dragonfly heard a low faint hum,
an echo of sonar, deep within the sea.
Waves and tides rushing in and out.
The great leviathan spoke
to the dragonfly,
remember the way, the many paths
and tracts you've journeyed.

Remember you've experienced
much of life and earned your
freedom to transform,
manifest and fly to new places,
with love, joy, happiness
and peace in your heart.

The courage and strength to adapt.
You shape shift, metamorphosis
and rise all your own doing.
Hard won lessons and truths
echo from the deep sonar
calling out to you now.

You desire to dip your wings
into the water, to touch
ever so gently the surface.
A desire you've not known before -
yet it resonates within every fiber
of your dragonfly being,
home.

A knowing so strong,
it's like a great migration
push and pull, magnetic,
physical, spiritual, chemical
alchemy at its purest.

Driven by the moon
and tides themselves,
that the water has visioned
and brought up from
the deep blue sea.
The dragonfly heard
the whale and leviathan's sonar
calls so deeply
that she flew ever so swiftly
to the water's surface.
Sun rays glistened
a golden sheen so bright,
they emerged as one in a flash
of brilliance and illusion.

Divine intervention.
The dragonfly of flight,
melded and merged with
the knowing flow of
the azure, blue ocean.
Joy, happiness.
Peace, and love.

19

I AM THAT BLUE WAVE

I am that blue wave
rising at your shore.
Rolling in and out,
constant, rhythmic,
consistent, forceful.

I am that blue wave
crashing and reverberating
with successive thuds
at your shore.

I am that blue wave
you saw far out in the distance
on the horizon,
rolling in towards you
with sureness and devotion.

I am that blue wave
coming towards you,
rolling over and over
at your shore,
open and vulnerable.

I am that blue wave
capsizing at your shore,
saltwater spray in the air
white, foamy, frothy,
suds from my energy
dissipating everywhere.

I am that blue wave
you hear at night in the dark,
all night long in your dreams
constantly, rhythmically,
turning over onto your shore.

I am that blue wave
that can lift your spirits
with joy and laughter-
gently holding you
in my surf of water.

I am that blue wave
moved by the full moons.
I appear and recede
with the tides of my love
to your shore.

I am that blue rogue wave
that pushes your air
above me to its limits,
spraying my saltiness
everywhere.

I am that blue wave
that cannot be controlled,
contained, nor predicted.
In motion,
yet I am constantly
coming back to your shore.

I am that blue wave
that happily rushes in to greet you
no matter where you are
every time.

I am that blue wave
that cannot cease my motion
towards your shore.
The tidal pull of fate and destiny
is too strong to ignore.

I am that blue wave
that rises in height and cadence
towards your shore,
in anticipation of rushing in
to see you, your home!

I am that blue wave,
I am water,
H20.

20

SNEAKER WAVE

For many blue moons now,
the blue star-spangled dragonfly
has been as busy as a zephyr
flying overhead.
Zipping back and forth
over the deep blue sea.
Her energy and cadence
increasing in vigor and speed.

She's driven by a passion
to be united with her dolphin
in their spiral dance.
A moment suspended
in time and space,
that comes every few weeks
with the tides.

She anticipates and waits
for these moments
to be free at last
with her dolphin.
So too the dolphin,
who anticipates and circles
below the water's surface
in the ocean blue
waiting to be with her dragonfly too.

Suddenly the wind and weather changes.
The winds in a gale force frenzy
whip up the blue water,
unfurling a giant outpouring
of a sneaker wave
far beyond the shore.

The blue wave flows
further up the coast

than ever before
with great speed and determination.
It captures
the blue star-spangled dragonfly
and dolphin in their spiral dance.

They are transformed
rolling deep within the water tube
of the sneaker wave.
United with a passion,
flowing wildly
to their destiny and fate,
roaring in the blue waves.
Powerful surf,
time suspended in joy,
happiness, peace and love.
Air and water unleashed,
free at last to go with the flow
to a destination only they know.

21

SPIRAL DANCE

It all started the day
the dolphin/ lil' fish jumped out
of the sea and into the air
to help and support Tammy B.
Transformed as the dolphin/lil' fish
saw the dragonfly in the sunshine.
Blinded by the shimmering light.
Hearing the whale's song,
sung by sonar from
the depths of ocean blue.

It was a lullaby of the tides
carried for Team Blue.
Destiny and fate calling out to you.
A snake slithered on the sand,
the magician at work
transmuting and changing
old habits and fears discarded.
Leaving its skin on the sand,
a sign.

A lizard crawled past
discarded snake skin on the beach,
where fear once followed.
Paying attention to the dreams
and remembering the way.
It was after a tiny spider for a meal.
An opportunity or gift to be given
by an infinite being so small,
with a legacy of expansive fate.

The dolphin/lil' fish saw all this
through her fisheyes.
Total view with an immediate reply,
a vision.

The Great Spirit said
we are all one and connected.
You are to bring support
and love to others.
Break free from the water barriers
fly free in the air, lil' flying fish,
it's in your dreams.

Manifestation of fears and desire.
I now know my life force is within me!
It's joy, happiness, peace and love.
A great gift from heaven above.
The dolphin/lil' fish did a spiral dance
above the water and in the air!

22

THE BLUE WAVE UNFURLS

He said it didn't matter
race, creed, color or origin.
You see when I left
and came back from over there
no one really cared.
He said it didn't matter
man or woman,
gay or straight
and it's okay to be
LGBTQ you.
It's not up for debate.
He said it's not about
if you are able bodied
or if you're colorblind.
It's just time to give
all you got
from your own table
to help, love and support
Kamala Harris.
He said
I will put the words
in your hand
and you will put
that blue pen to paper.
He said you see
you are one of my arrows
in my mighty quiver.
I have held you
and others back
like a great dam.
The time is now
to release the water.
He said your life is
about love and kindness
it will freely flow
from the watery depths

of your heart and soul.
I was overtaken
by a blue wave of beauty
then I rushed in to release
 my blue pen to paper.
With each breath
and blue pen stroke
I exhaled a sigh of relief.
What is it like to feel
an African American woman
could finally be the "Chief?
I exhaled, AIR
Love and devotion
unfurled a giant blue wave
that stirred and swept
across the ocean blue.
He said it's true
your hopes and dreams
can come true.
Remember the way.

23

THE BLUE WAVE OF DEVOTION

In your eyes I see
the cool blue pools of water
reflected at me.
It seems like remembering
back to eternity.
I've been waiting for you
to roll back to my shore.

Like the blue wave at the ocean,
I return to your shore
over and over again.
Waiting for you to receive
my love and devotion.

The time has finally come.
Where once you had doubts
and needed to be sure.
Weary of being captured
in a net of lies
you couldn't escape.
Such was the harm
and trauma
of past mistakes.
Not knowing
which way to turn.
Yet all along
your true, blue heart
yearned for the water
that you knew
would comfort, sustain
and give you
new growth for life.

So, there I stood,
and you were feelin' good.
Here I am, that you know

and can trust.
I am true, blue goodness
forged from high sea storms.
Listen to your heart and
the power of the cosmic law
of universal love.
Shadow and light, inside and out.
Now's the time to
believe what's in your heart.

To me there is no doubt.
The calm, blue water like glass,
mirroring the depths of
your water tiger's heart and soul.
You are pure white light
to the core.
I see your beauty
and purpose goes far beyond.

You are the Bonnie
to my Clyde.
The ying to my yang.
Thelma to my Louise.
The desert to my heart.
The song you sing,
I hear, want and need.
You stayed the course
and true to yourself,
you had no choice
but to stay and work it out.
Finally, the fear and apprehension
that once tossed you about
in a frothy fury subsides.

Do you now see?
I am that cool, blue wave of water
returning to your shore.
Rolling over and over again,
devoted to you.
With a lifelong sureness
that promises to never
break your tender heart.

I'd rather go blind.
But you've watched the waves
and searched your soul in vain.
It is so complex and
not logical to explain.

The heart wants what it wants.

Funny how we are right
where we are meant to be.
Destiny and fate
washing you back to me.
Patiently waiting.
Is it true, a blue wave can wait?

Now or never. It is not too late.
I am that blue wave
returning to your shore.
Rolling over and over again.
Waiting for you to accept
and receive my love and devotion.
And I you.

For you see, it is simple
and all about what god put in motion.
The true, blue wave is really
full of love and devotion

24

THE LIL BLUE M&M

Today I was at the pool
doing my water therapy.
I am disabled with CRPS,
heart failure and spina bifida.
I am here
rewiring my brain and body.
Healing from
these illnesses and disabilities.
Not allowing those words
to define me or own me.

I see you there
with your mom
taking your first swim lesson
at age two.
Little Cindy Lou
Who is so bold.
Your blonde hair in a ponytail
on top of your head.
Dog paddling
towards your mom.
Full of life and love.
Smile on your face.
Joy and happiness
splashing everywhere.

I remember my mom
with me, age three.
Lake Mendota, Warner Park beach
and my first swim lessons.
The blue water.
The slapping of the waves
at the sandy shore.
The expansive lakeview
beyond the horizon.
The silky touch of the water

on my skin and body.
The birds singing
from the trees nearby.
The wind on my face
and sun in my eyes.
It was fun.
It was joy, happiness,
peace and love.

I think of my mother's love
and yours.
How moms are there
from the start
teaching us everything
from their hearts.
How to feel safe
and live life.
Breath and relax.
Eat and drink. Rest and sleep.
Talk and walk. Play and pray.

My love of water is owed
to my mom that day.
She made sure
I got those lessons
and learned to swim.
By god, no matter what.
I didn't know then
that she feared water.
She never learned to swim.
Her mother just didn't care.
There was no reason nor love.

Today as I swim
in the sea of life with you,
I think about how
I used to define myself
saying I'm disabled
with these medical conditions.
My mom taught me that too.
No more.

I choose to send those words
and script packing.
I am healing inside and out
from all those medical conditions.
I am the little
blue miracle in motion (M&M)

swimming in the waters of life.
It feels like Joy,
happiness, peace and love.

YOU SPOKE TO ME

You spoke to me in the waves
at the azure, blue ocean.
Your powers unfurled,
air plus H2O.

Swells, pounding hearts,
methodical melodies of forces
unfurling before me,
thuds, splashes, suds and foam,
hissing and swirling, reverberations
and vibrations of chemical energy,
fluid and expansive, ripples and effect.
Little did I know
the magic at work.
We united for a greater good.

Undulating waves, hypnotic currents,
colors that reflected and
mirrored our sparkling blue eyes.
Splashed before me,
playfully reminding me of joy,
happiness, peace and love.
All that matters for all of us.
The fullness of the ocean,
endless, boundless, freely flowing,
independent, at its source
and everywhere.

Air and all that you breathe.
You are purrrfection to me!
Absolutely stunningly beautiful,
radiant, magnificent being.
You glow like the moonlight
cast on the sea.
The brightest white light.
Omg!

26

AIR TO MY WATER

A dragonfly came to me
at Salmo Pond, as I was
in the water today.
I was thinking of you
floating and feeling my body,
legs, back, arms, feet, belly.

At 7PM the winds blew.
The aspen leaves quaking
and a dragonfly came to me
in the water. Hovering still.
Observing me from
a short distance,

It's you!
Just what you do, my Aquarius.
It's your way.
I said hello to you.
I said I can't wait
to finally see you.
At last it shall be,
time is irrelevant
it stands still
when we meet.

I just know what I know.
I feel your warmth.
I see your eyes, that smile.
I hear your throaty chortle.
My loins and breasts ache for you.
You dart about.
Your playful side is
otherworldly to me!
Enchantress.

I feel your desire

my core muscles tense,
my stomach seizes
my heart explodes with love!
You're sending me your air,
soft erotic touches on the winds.
I feel you.

27

AIR YOU TOUCHED ME

At dawn from the east,
the enchantress of the air.
You gently,
ever so softly,
whisper in my ear
on the morning mists.

In daylight,
you laugh
and your wind playfully
tickles my belly

At sunset,
with the energy
you have built from the day,
you send gusts of wind
and heat that I happily greet.

At night,
your calm winds blow
as darkness falls.
A smooth, silky, erotic breeze
brings me to my knees.

At midnight,
you send a breeze
to swoon and swirl me
in my dreams.
Air you touched me.

28

BATHE YOU IN MY WATER

Let me bath you
in the cool blue
waters of my eyes.

Let me shine
like a moonlit sea before you,
iridescent
and mirroring your beauty.

Let me move your soul
with my watery currents
of joy, happiness,
peace, and love.

Let me wash over you
in a wave of my Irish heather scent,
filling your lungs
with a hunger for more.

Let me gently rock you
with my waves of affection
so that you know
you are puurrrfect to me,
as you are.

Let me buoy you up
to go the distance at sea
to reach your
blue wave goal.

Let me be your maiden ship
and you the pirate
who sets your sails high
full of my life force.

Let me be your dolphin friend.

We can play
and have fun out at sea.

Let me bring you seashells
and treasures from faraway places,
encouraging you to
not fear the adventure,
and the future ahead.

Let me be your mermaid,
fish and woman in one,
so you can dream
of the oceans of life.
Eternal, everlasting blue.

Let me be your lil fish Pisces
and shower you
with my watery love.

29

FEELING LIKE A DINOSAUR

You know you are getting old when,
the young people you are mentoring
tell you you're the same age
as their parents and joke
they have to wear reading glasses too.

You know you are getting old when,
you survived the death of a spouse
or divorce,
and you still think there is time
to find the "right one"
to live happily ever after with.

You know you are getting old when,
you got more age spots
on your body
than freckles in your youth.

You know you are getting old when,
you attempt 30-foot ski jump
as if your body was 20 again.
You crash and burn,
breaking bones,
wondering why it happened?

You know you are getting old when,
your energy level for the day
peaks at 11 AM
and you're ready for a nap at 1PM.

You know you are getting old when,
your body shape resembles
the Grinch or a Smurf.
Not an hourglass or a tripod.

You know you are getting old when,

your exercise routine consists of
going to work for 8 hours a day
and you're too exhausted to do
anything else when you get home
but nap.

You know you are getting old when,
you wonder how you got so old so fast
and how come no one told you
it would be this way.

30

GRATEFUL

See the beauty all around you.

If you only had one day to live,
what would you do with it?
If you only had an hour to live,
who would you choose to be with?

It doesn't matter if
your life is hard or easy work.
Change comes for us all.
Trust in divine intervention
or call it destiny and fate.
You are here for a reason.

It doesn't matter
what material stuff you gather,
we all know you can't take it with you.
It doesn't matter what others say,
the constant chatter and gossip.
That's fear and hate.
You will rise up and they know it.

Divine forces are
behind every glow up,
the sign you chose
wisely with a pure heart.
The blow ups are karmic lessons
repeated until you get it right.

So glow up or glow down?
You choose and know your heart.
There are always signs
if you look around.

It's the air you breathe
that gives you life.
It's the water you taste

that makes you whole.
See the beauty and love
all around you.

The divine truly wants
the highest and best for you.
Did you ever think
you'd make it this far?
Start your day slow,
say a prayer and be grateful
you are still breathing AIR.
Feel your every heart beat
and breath of AIR.
Be peaceful and aware
as you go out into your world.
Every cell of your body vibrates
with divine energy.

Even Einstein identified LOVE
as energy.
The chemistry we feel with
certain people
is always for a reason.
A sign.

See the beauty all around you.
Be grateful you come alive with,
WATER + AIR .
Let the seed be planted there

31

HIGH ANXIETY

Living in Cross Plains.
Working at a crossroads cafe.
She tells me
she don't know
what she should do.
Yet she's working at the ranch
and the cafe too.
It seems to me
she's got plenty to do.
Maybe it's
the convergence of space and time
that's got her internal compass
all askew.
From where I'm standing,
she's got it all
and my love too.

32

HOW YOU MAKE ME FEEL

I am a Pisces, water.
I feel and intuit
every nonverbal cue and gesture.
Every glance or blink of your eyes.
Every nod or tilt of your head.
Every shift or position of your body.
Every flick of your hair
and lick of your lips.
Every gentle touch to my hand or body.
Every breath.

Inhale my scent and exhale.
I hear your release in peace.
Seeing you is like a blue wave at the ocean.
I see you coming in towards me.
I smell you in the air, salty and sensual.
I hear that constant echo,
rumble, and reverberation
inside my body as you approach.
I feel deep within that past connection
and spiritual knowingness of the emerald
Azure, blue aura of you, Aquarius.
Unfurling before me.

You rush in on the wave
and in the wind.
I greet you with such joy,
happiness, peace, and love.
I've been waiting for you
to arrive at my shore.
We touch hands and hug.

I feel a splash
as our energies playfully unite.
I let you pour all over my body
from head to toe.

It makes me so happy
to see and feel you,
air, Aquarius!

Then you have to retreat,
leave, go elsewhere.
It's your job, I know it well.
So I'll patiently await the arrival
of the next roll
of your blue wave.

33

I ADORE YOU

I adore your eyes
From the very first time
I saw you there
I got lost in
your beautiful blue eyes.
You were
that ethereal rainbow queen
staring back at me.
I've been waiting all my life
to see that light in your eyes.
It truly was love at first sight.

I adore your smile
From the very first time
I saw your smile as wide as
a country mile.
You were loving,
gentle, and kind.
I've been waiting all my life
to see your bright white
megawatt smile shine on me.
It truly was love at first sight.

I adore your hugs
From that very first
warm embrace,
you wrapped me up in love
and held me oh so tight.
You were so full of warmth,
and it felt so right
letting you hold me tight.
I been waiting all my life
to hold a girl like you,
and feel the power
of love's might.
It truly was love at first sight.

I adore your scent
From that very first time
I inhaled your scent
as you breathed in mine.
You were so intoxicating
full of life's sweetness.
I been waiting all my life
to breathe you in
and the smell of your skin.
It was truly love at first sight.

I adore your voice
From that very first time
I heard your voice,
it was a serene lullaby
that brought tears to my eyes.
You were so full of calm,
it soothed my worries and storms.
I been waiting all of my life
to hear those sweet words
fall from your lips,
l love you.
It truly was love at first sight.

I adore your heartbeat
From that very first time I felt
your heartbeat go boom, boom,
next to mine. I knew it was divine.
You were so full of chemistry
and energy
it was the alchemy of destiny
and fate.
I been waiting all my life
to feel a heartbeat
as deep and soulful as mine.
It truly was true love at first sight.

34

I'M IN LOVE WITH AIR

Aquarius, fixed sign, winds of time,
Dragonfly, transforming
before my eyes.
You found me,
the Dolphin in the blue sea,
Our chemistry overpowering.
We both did a double take,
it was that compelling.

We both sniffed the air.
You more than I.
A habit on the hunts,
check the air.
I sensed it empathically.
The body language
and nonverbal cues
that went without notice.
You, less sensitive due to public life
and being overwhelmed
with bodies and crowds.
You are numb to it.
But I felt your emotions
and heart in an instant.

Then the tactile cues
and touch.
The showing of teeth
and a smile.
The eyes wide open alert
to friend or foe.
Once you figured out
the chemistry was there,
it never left your inner world
for months.
Something is up.

Feelings you can't explain.
Songs you recognize.
Hints in daily life.
Time and space warping.
Synchronicity at play.
I've visioned you and me.
I've manifested in my dreams
the 'We'.
I've hoped and prayed
you'd awaken, too.
The playfulness I exuded to capture
your eyes and heart.
I've put my cards on the table,
my humility.
Do I lack tact?
Do I lack decorum?
Am I embarrassing you?
Am I frustrating you?
Am I pleasing you?
Without your reply, how will I know?
Time is precious to me now.
I wished you'd call or speak to me!

35

I'M ONLY

I'm only
alright when
I get to be with you.
I'm only
good when you are
near me.
I'm only
relaxed knowing
you've got my back.
I'm only
able to breathe
deeply with your arms
wrapped around me.
I'm only
able to see clearly
when you look at me
in that way.
I'm only
okay and know
the way to go
when you say the things
that you say.
I'm only
hearing my heartbeat
when you sing your song.
I'm only
safe at night
when you're in my dreams.
I'm only
free to let it all go
with the flow
when you ignite
that fire within me.
I'm only
here today
because you make me feel

loved and understood.
I'm only
good with you
true blue.

36

LISTEN, SHHH

Listen, shhhh...
Can you see
the sparks igniting
between you and me?

Listen, shhh...
Can you smell
my cologne swirl
in an intoxicating mix
around you?

Listen, shhh...
Can you touch
the fire of desire
as we pull close?

Listen, shhh...
Can you hear
the passion sing
from our lips
as we speak?

Listen, shhh...
Can you feel
the drumbeat of
our hearts love
as we embrace?

Listen, shhh...
Can this be
destiny and fate
in true love's wake?

37

ROAD TRIP MADE IN WISCONSIN

It begins with the green and gold.
Packer up. Wisconsin style.
So excited we're gonna hit the road
in Bad Betty, my 65 Ford F100.
Time for a Wisconsin road trip
up north with you.
Yah, hey!

We're flying along on Highway 51,
more true blue than Route 66.
Listening to the radio sing our song.
Heading up to
Hodag Country Music Festival.
To hear Jelly Roll sing
about how he found
his way home too.
Thinking about all the veterans
who gave us all they had,
including my dad.
For freedom.

God has blessed the USA.
Driving past
Wisconsin dairy farms.
Nothing but
black n white Holstein cows
as far as I can see.
Those farmers' grandfathers,
the boys in blue,
fought for me and you.
They built farms,
businesses and homes
in freedom loving Wisconsin.
True blue ones.

The miles and days roll by

as I'm looking at
the black n white.
You're riding shotgun
with your blonde hair
blowing in the wind.
I look over at you
and thank the Lord for
the day he created
his best true blue, you!
That megawatt killer smile.
Blue eyes that sparkle
like diamonds
and a heart of gold.
I never met anyone so bold.

It ain't long now and
we're in the big trees.
We passed through
the glacial tension zone,
to days gone by
of loggers and lumberjacks.
They did the hard work
to clear and take back
the land so we could eat,
thrive, and survive.
All on Babe, the Blue Ox's back.

I steal a glimpse over at you
and get lost in watery ocean blue eyes.
As we arrive at our destination,
that log cabin on the lake,
I can't help but thank God and Team Blue
for the clean lake of water too.
Finally, to be up north
on this lake with you.
I can't wait to toast a sweet glass of
Wollersheim wine
with you.
It is true blue.

Any Wisconsin road trip
in Bad Betty
is God's plan coming true,
for me and you.

38

THE MIGHTY ONE KAMALA HARRIS

She rolled in on the blue wave

to Madison, Wisconsin.
On the eve of the fall equinox
and the season of Libra.
Equality, focus and perspective
on full display.
Her presence represents
the scales of justice in fluid motion.
A delicate balance of
night and day, dark and light,
feminine and masculine, inside and out,
love vs hate.
The 80,000+ souls of true-blue ocean
surrounding and buoying her
with a hermetic pulse.
Illuminating and mirroring that
universal force washing back to her.
Unseen energy
but true blue as the waters of life.
Her message like water calm,
clear and smooth.
Have faith and courage as you flow about
for you only have one life to lose
for our country, the good old USA
So you better make it count.
The blue water absorbed the music
playing like a great storm
whipped to a frenzy and
washing us all about.
Water droplets dancing in
the rains of hope and freedom.
Rockin and rollin together
united for a purpose greater than ourselves.
The blue wave she crested
in confidence, with persistence
and was steadfast

in overtaking all of the souls in her path.
As the blue wave passed
the water reflected back an inner knowledge
 that only the heart carries
when aligned with one's purpose.
It is true,
the blue water can transform life
with LOVE & KINDNESS.

39

SUNSTONES GUIDE THE WAY

Many nights and days
I've been adrift
on the big blue sea.
Searching for my pirate tiger
Using the sunstones
of the Viking ships
to stay the course.

It's been several weeks
since I last saw you.
How iridescent
and beautiful you are
golden fleece hair
flowing in twilight wind.
Illumination so divine,
frozen in time.
Your smile engulfs me
like a blue wave.
Wider than
a country mile
making that two hour drive
all the more worthwhile!

I found you there
using the ancient communication
between moon and stars.
Sunstones bright enough
to bring us there.
Those heaven-sent
celestial messages guiding
the pirate ship closer to you.
Thy will be done
not mine.

Was it destiny and fate?
I'm glad I wasn't late.

How grateful I was
to see you there,
my friend of the air.
Couldn't wait to wrap you
in my watery waves
hold you suspended
with gentle eternal care.
You now know
its joy, happiness, peace
and love.
Time stood still
but a moment.
Who could miss
that 1000 watt illuminating
pirate tiger smile?
For you there's no question.
I'd walk 1000 miles!

The photo says it all.
Gratitude.
Grateful for that moment
ever so small.
To behold the beauty
when two water tigers meet
and stand so tall.
United at last
once and for all.

I thank God for
those sunstones
that guided my way
and I pray I will see
my pirate on the blue sea
another day!
Alas, the pirate ship
is safe and sound
on the big blue sea,
where she is adrift
but not aground.
Funny how
the smallest gestures
can be so profound!

40

YOU ARE MY OCEAN BLUE

At last,
I've come to the ocean blue air.
Your winds and surf pound,
thud, reverberate in powerful surges
at my shore.

My chest feels the pounding
in the waves
of your winged heartbeat as it
meets mine.

Elemental, ancient,
constant, receptive,
feminine, successive,
sureness.
My azure eyes shine.
They mirror back the
ever-iridescent blues and
aquamarines of your eyes too.
The seat of your soul
calls out to mine
like a leviathan's sonar call.

I hear you.
I want to spiral dance
with you in joy,
happiness, peace and love.
The frothy white foamy suds
formed by the mixing of air
and water.
Two water tigers,
our powers united.
Only a moment in time.

Eternal bonds and connections
with the alchemy of air and water

summoned up from the depths
of the blue ocean,
unfurl in the winds at your shore.
Tsunami energy with faith.
Thy will be done, not mine.

Creativity unleashed
unfurling in a blue wave
of childlike wonders.
Can this be real and true?
Seashells, sea glass, sea horses,
sea turtles, sea creatures,
sea kelpies, sand dollars.
All the blue ocean gifts.

A sense of wonder and possibilities
are rising out of the deep blue sea.
You are the air over my ocean blue.
It's Home. Gratitude.

41

WISCONSIN VISION

Down that same road
at sunset to where?
Do you know?
Down where the sun
goes home.
Or will you try
to go up in the sky?
Where the eagles fly
in the morning sun rise.
Above and below,
So it goes.
Divine light guides you,
Either way.
Follow your heart.

ABOUT THE AUTHOR

Penni Klein is a fourth-generation Wisconsin native and retired Public Lands Recreation and Forestry Director. Penni's education includes a B.S. from the University of Wisconsin in Natural Resources Management/Forestry. Her natural curiosity and adventure in the outdoors were fed by involvement with horses, BlackHawk Girls Scouts, Cherokee Marsh School projects, East High School FFA Agriculture, and YCC/WCC. Penni's natural curiosity and drive led her to work at the national, state, county, and city levels, gaining a deep understanding of how these systems worked. Her career took her to: Dane County Parks (including the Glacial Drumlin Trail), Peninsula State Park, Rocky Mountain National Park, Perrot State Park, Great River Trail, Kettle Moraine State Forest Northern Unit, Devil's Lake, Governor Nelson State Park, and City of Middleton. Penni's skillset is varied and includes experience as a Parks Superintendent, a Park Ranger, a Conservation Warden with her Law Enforcement Certification. She is also an ADA and equine therapy disabilities advocate. Penni enjoys any and all water related activities that bring her life. As a descendent of a long line of progressively-minded farm family members, Penni hopes to inspire others by sharing her writings. *Ride the Blue Wave* is her first published book of poems, highlighting themes of mirrored reflection in the various presentations of land, water, wildlife, and Wisconsin politics. Penni's primary inspirations for her poems include nature and water. Penni is an out and proud member of the LGBTQIA+ community. She resides in Dane County, Madison, in the Blue heart of Wisconsin with her beloved cat, Bootsie.